Blue Crab Publishing

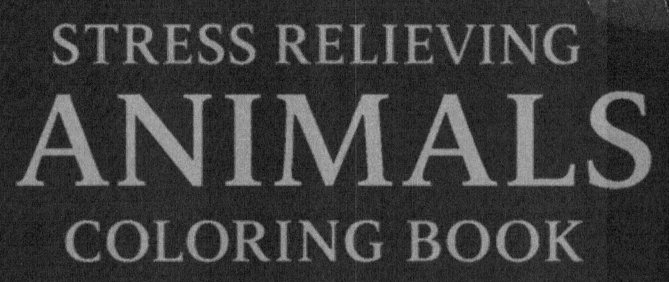

STRESS RELIEVING
ANIMALS
COLORING BOOK

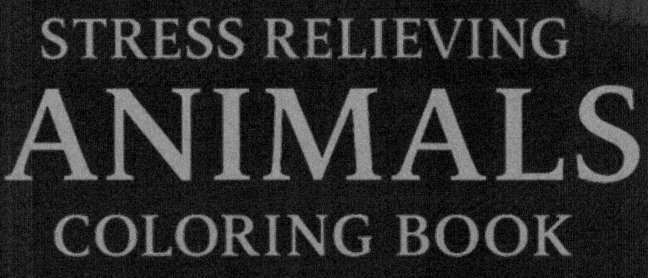

STRESS RELIEVING
ANIMALS
COLORING BOOK

STRESS RELIEVING
ANIMALS
COLORING BOOK

STRESS RELIEVING
ANIMALS
COLORING BOOK

STRESS RELIEVING
ANIMALS
COLORING BOOK

STRESS RELIEVING
ANIMALS
COLORING BOOK

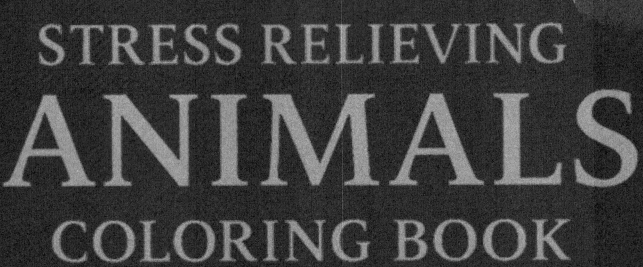

STRESS RELIEVING
ANIMALS
COLORING BOOK

STRESS RELIEVING
ANIMALS
COLORING BOOK

STRESS RELIEVING
ANIMALS
COLORING BOOK

STRESS RELIEVING
ANIMALS
COLORING BOOK

STRESS RELIEVING
ANIMALS
COLORING BOOK

STRESS RELIEVING
ANIMALS
COLORING BOOK

STRESS RELIEVING
ANIMALS
COLORING BOOK

STRESS RELIEVING
ANIMALS
COLORING BOOK

Thank you for reading my book. Please, don't forget your review on Amazon. A small gesture for you but very important for me.

Scan this QR code if you want to receive the bonus.

Follow us on social media.

Printed in Great Britain
by Amazon